a taste of
chocolate

THE AUSTRALIAN
Women's Weekly

contents

This book is a chocoholic's dream come true in the wonderful textures and colours of rich dark, creamy milk and sweet white chocolate. There are dazzling desserts, tantalising treats, stunning little gift ideas and cakes and pastries of all shapes and sizes in varying degrees of decadent gooiness. The recipes are sure to impress and delight the most discerning lovers of chocolate.

Pamela Clark

Food Director

Ever since the Aztecs first tasted the fruit of the cocoa tree, we haven't been able to resist chocolate. Its smooth sensual taste seduces the taste buds in rich cakes, creamy desserts, chewy brownies and sumptuous tea-time treats. These divine recipes range from the decadent to the delicate.

chocolate crowned sticky date cakes

120g dark eating chocolate,
  melted
1¾ cups (250g) seeded
  dried dates
1 teaspoon bicarbonate of soda
1 cup (250ml) boiling water
60g butter, chopped
¾ cup (165g) firmly packed
  brown sugar
2 eggs
1 cup (150g) self-raising flour
80g dark eating chocolate,
  chopped coarsely
chocolate butterscotch sauce
½ cup (110g) firmly packed
  brown sugar
⅔ cup (160ml) cream
50g butter
1 tablespoon cocoa powder, sifted

1 Preheat oven to 180°C/160°C fan-forced. Grease 6-hole texas (¾ cup/180ml) muffin pan; line bases with baking paper.
2 Spread melted chocolate over base of each pan hole; refrigerate until set.
3 Meanwhile, combine dates, soda and the water in food processor, put lid in position; stand 5 minutes. Process until smooth. Add butter and sugar; process until combined. Add eggs and flour; pulse until combined. Stir in chopped chocolate.
4 Divide mixture among pan holes; bake about 15 minutes. Stand cakes 2 minutes; turn onto wire rack to cool slightly. Remove paper.
5 Make chocolate butterscotch sauce.
6 Serve warm cakes drizzled with sauce and whipped cream, if you like.
chocolate butterscotch sauce
Stir ingredients in medium saucepan over heat, without boiling, until sugar dissolves; bring to the boil. Remove from heat.

makes 6

ginger chocolate creams

125g unsalted butter, softened
⅓ cup (75g) firmly packed
   brown sugar
2 tablespoons golden syrup
½ cup (75g) self-raising flour
⅔ cup (100g) wholemeal
   self-raising flour
1 teaspoon ground ginger
1 tablespoon cocoa powder
chocolate ginger cream
¼ cup (60ml) cream
150g milk eating chocolate,
   chopped coarsely
¼ cup (55g) finely chopped
   glacé ginger

1 Beat butter and sugar in small bowl with electric mixer until light and fluffy. Beat in golden syrup. Stir in sifted dry ingredients, in two batches. Knead on floured surface until smooth.
2 Roll dough between sheets of baking paper until 5mm thick; refrigerate 30 minutes.
3 Meanwhile, make chocolate ginger cream.
4 Preheat oven to 180°C/160°C fan-forced. Grease two oven trays; line with baking paper.
5 Cut 32 x 5.5cm rounds from dough; place on trays.
6 Bake biscuits about 5 minutes; cool on trays. Sandwich biscuits with chocolate ginger cream.
chocolate ginger cream Stir cream and chocolate in small heatproof bowl over small saucepan of simmering water until smooth. Stir in ginger; refrigerate until spreadable.

makes 16

cardamom orange mousse cakes

50g dark eating chocolate, melted
25g unsalted butter, melted
125g butternut snap biscuits
25g unsalted butter,
   melted, extra
1 teaspoon finely grated
   orange rind
¼ teaspoon ground cardamom
orange mousse
300ml thickened cream
150g dark eating chocolate,
   chopped coursely
1 teaspoon finely grated
   orange rind
¼ teaspoon ground cardamom
orange syrup
⅔ cup (160ml) orange juice
¼ cup (55g) caster sugar
2 tablespoons finely shredded
   orange rind

1 Make orange mousse.
2 Grease 12-hole (¼ cup/60ml) mini cheesecake pan with removable bases; line bases with baking paper.
3 Combine chocolate and butter, spoon into holes; cool 5 minutes.
4 Process biscuits until fine. Add extra butter, rind and cardamom; process until combined. Divide mixture among pan holes; press firmly over chocolate bases.
5 Divide mousse among pan holes; refrigerate overnight.
6 Make orange syrup.
7 Serve mousse cakes with orange syrup.

orange mousse Stir ingredients in small heatproof bowl over small saucepan of simmering water until smooth. Refrigerate about 30 minutes or until cool. Beat mousse mixture with electric mixer for 2 minutes or until mixture changes to a paler colour. Do not overbeat or mixture will curdle.

orange syrup Stir juice and sugar in small saucepan, over heat, without boiling, until sugar dissolves. Add rind; bring to the boil. Reduce heat; simmer, uncovered, about 10 minutes or until syrup thickens slightly. Cool.

makes 12

chocolate shortbread stars

250g unsalted butter, softened
1 cup (160g) icing sugar
1¼ cups (185g) plain flour
½ cup (100g) rice flour
¼ cup (25g) cocoa powder
60g (125) dark Choc Bits
2 tablespoons icing sugar, extra

1 Beat butter and sugar in medium bowl with electric mixer until light and fluffy. Stir in sifted flours and cocoa, in two batches. Knead on floured surface until smooth. Roll dough between sheets of baking paper until 1cm thick; refrigerate 30 minutes.
2 Preheat oven to 160°C/140°C fan-forced. Grease two oven trays; line with baking paper.
3 Cut 25 x 6.5cm stars from dough. Place stars about 4cm apart on trays. Decorate with Choc Bits.
4 Bake stars about 20 minutes; cool on trays. Dust stars with extra sifted icing sugar.

makes 25

185g unsalted butter, softened
¾ cup (165g) firmly packed
  brown sugar
1¼ cups (185g) plain flour
⅓ cup (65g) finely chopped
  dried figs
½ cup (60g) finely chopped
  roasted pecans
½ cup (95g) dark Choc Bits
100g dark eating chocolate,
  melted

1 Preheat oven to 180°C/160°C fan-forced. Grease 20cm x 30cm lamington pan; line base with baking paper, extending paper 5cm over long sides.
2 Beat butter and sugar in small bowl with electric mixer until light and fluffy. Stir in sifted flour, then figs, nuts and Choc Bits. Press mixture into pan.
3 Bake slice about 25 minutes. Mark slice into 24 squares. Cool slice in pan; drizzle with chocolate. Cut into squares when chocolate is set.

makes 24

choc-chip, fig and pecan slice

pom poms

395g can sweetened
   condensed milk
30g unsalted butter
1 cup (140g) finely chopped
   roasted unsalted peanuts
4 cups (40g) air-popped popcorn
½ cup (40g) toasted shredded
   coconut
200g milk eating chocolate,
   melted

1 Line two trays with baking paper.
2 Combine condensed milk and butter in large heavy-based saucepan; cook, stirring, over medium heat, about 10 minutes or until mixture is a caramel colour. Remove from heat; quickly stir in nuts, popcorn and coconut.
3 Working quickly, roll walnut-sized pieces of mixture into balls. Dip balls in chocolate; place on trays. Refrigerate until firm.

makes 40

chocolate hazelnut thins

1 egg white
¼ cup (55g) brown sugar
2 tablespoons plain flour
2 teaspoons cocoa powder
30g butter, melted
1 teaspoon milk
1 tablespoon hazelnut meal

1 Preheat oven to 180°C/160°C fan-forced. Grease oven trays.
2 Beat egg white in small bowl with electric mixer until soft peaks form; gradually add sugar, beating until sugar dissolves. Stir in sifted flour and cocoa, then butter, milk and hazelnut meal.
3 Spread level teaspoons of mixture into 8cm circles, about 4cm apart on trays.
4 Bake thins, in batches, about 5 minutes. Remove from tray immediately using metal spatula, place over rolling pin to cool (see page 112).

makes 24

chocolate churros

60g unsalted butter
⅔ cup (160ml) water
1⅓ cups (200g) plain flour
2 tablespoons cocoa powder
1½ tablespoons caster sugar
2 eggs
vegetable oil, for deep-frying
½ cup (110g) white sugar
2 tablespoons cocoa powder,
    extra

1 Combine butter and the water in medium saucepan; bring to the boil. Add sifted flour, cocoa and caster sugar; beat with wooden spoon over high heat until mixture comes away from base and side of pan to form a smooth ball. Transfer mixture to small bowl; beat in eggs, one at a time, with electric mixer until mixture becomes glossy.
2 Spoon mixture into piping bag fitted with a 1.5cm fluted tube.
3 Heat oil in deep pan or wok; pipe 7cm lengths of batter into oil (cut off lengths with a knife). Deep-fry churros, in batches, about 6 minutes or until churros are crisp (see page 112). Drain on absorbent paper.
4 Roll churros in combined white sugar and sifted extra cocoa. Serve warm.

makes 14

chocolate, apricot and hazelnut cake

1⅔ cups (250g) dried apricots, chopped finely
½ cup (125ml) water
250g butter, softened
2 cups (440g) firmly packed brown sugar
6 eggs
1 cup (150g) plain flour
½ cup (75g) self-raising flour
¼ cup (25g) cocoa powder
1 cup (110g) hazelnut meal
⅔ cup (160ml) buttermilk
chocolate buttermilk cream
300g milk eating chocolate, chopped coarsely
½ cup (125ml) buttermilk
1 cup (160g) icing sugar

1 Combine apricots and the water in small saucepan; bring to the boil. Reduce heat; simmer, covered, stirring occasionally, about 10 minutes or until apricots are soft. Cool.
2 Preheat oven to 180°C/160°C fan-forced. Grease deep 22cm-round cake pan; line with baking paper.
3 Beat butter and sugar in small bowl with electric mixer until light and fluffy. Beat in eggs, one at a time. Transfer mixture to large bowl; stir in apricot mixture, sifted flours and cocoa, hazelnut meal and buttermilk, in two batches.
4 Spread mixture into pan; bake about 1 hour 50 minutes. Stand cake 10 minutes; turn, top-side up, onto wire rack to cool.

5 Meanwhile, make chocolate buttermilk cream.
6 Split cold cake into three layers; sandwich layers with two-thirds of the buttermilk cream. Spread cake with remaining buttermilk cream. Top with dark chocolate curls, if you like.
chocolate buttermilk cream
Stir chocolate and buttermilk in small heatproof bowl over small saucepan of simmering water until smooth; stir in sifted icing sugar. Refrigerate, stirring occasionally, about 30 minutes, or until spreadable.

serves 12

You will need 36 foil petit four cases for this recipe.

1 cup (150g) frozen raspberries, thawed
¼ cup (60ml) cream
2 tablespoons raspberry-flavoured liqueur
200g milk eating chocolate, chopped coarsely
36 frozen raspberries, extra

1 Push raspberries through a fine sieve into small heatproof bowl; discard seeds.
2 Add cream, liqueur and chocolate to bowl; stir over small saucepan of simmering water until smooth.
3 Divide half the chocolate mixture among cases; top with extra raspberries. Top with remaining chocolate mixture. Freeze truffles until firm.
4 Remove truffles from freezer 5 minutes before serving. Serve topped with edible gold leaf, if you like.

makes 36

frozen raspberry truffles

150g dark eating chocolate,
  chopped coarsely
⅓ cup (80ml) cream
40g unsalted butter
100g quince paste
¼ cup (35g) coarsely chopped
  roasted hazelnuts
pastry
¾ cup (110g) plain flour
¼ cup (25g) cocoa powder
¼ cup (40g) icing sugar
90g cold unsalted butter, chopped
1 egg yolk
1 tablespoon iced water,
  approximately

1 Make pastry.
2 Grease two 12-hole
(1½ tablespoons/30ml) shallow
round-based patty pans with
butter. Roll rounded teaspoons of
pastry into balls, press over base
and side of holes. Prick pastry
all over with fork. Refrigerate
30 minutes.
3 Preheat oven to 180°C/160°C
fan-forced.
4 Bake pastry cases 10 minutes.
5 Meanwhile, stir chocolate, cream
and butter in small heatproof bowl
over small saucepan of simmering
water until smooth. Cool 15 minutes.

6 Soften paste in microwave
oven on MEDIUM (75%) for about
20 seconds.
7 Divide paste among pastry cases;
top with half of the nuts. Top with
chocolate mixture, then remaining
nuts. Refrigerate 1 hour.
pastry Process sifted flour,
cocoa, icing sugar and butter until
crumbly. Add egg yolk and enough
of the water until ingredients just
come together when processed.
Knead dough on floured surface
until smooth. Enclose in plastic
wrap; refrigerate 30 minutes.

makes 24

chocolate, quince and hazelnut tartlets

warm malt truffle muffins

1¼ cups (185g) self-raising flour
¼ cup (30g) malted milk powder
2 tablespoons cocoa powder
pinch bicarbonate of soda
¼ cup (55g) brown sugar
60g unsalted butter
⅓ cup (125g) barley malt syrup
½ cup (125ml) milk
1 egg
¾ cup (180ml) cream
malt truffles
200g milk eating chocolate,
   chopped coarsely
¼ cup (60ml) cream
½ cup (60g) malted milk powder

1 Make malt truffles.
2 Preheat oven to 180°C/160°C fan-forced. Line 12-hole (⅓ cup/80ml) muffin pan with paper cases.
3 Sift flour, malt powder, cocoa, soda and sugar into medium bowl.
4 Stir butter and malt syrup in small saucepan over low heat until smooth.
5 Stir butter mixture, milk and egg into flour mixture. Do not over-mix; mixture should be lumpy. Divide half the mixture among cases. Place a truffle into each case; top with remaining mixture.
6 Bake muffins about 20 minutes; cool 2 minutes, then remove paper cases.
7 Meanwhile, stir reserved malt truffle mixture and cream in small saucepan, over low heat, until malt sauce is smooth.
8 Serve warm muffins with warm sauce. Dust with sifted cocoa powder, if you like.

malt truffles Stir ingredients in small heatproof bowl over small saucepan of simmering water until smooth. Reserve ½ cup (125ml) mixture for malt sauce. Refrigerate remaining mixture about 30 minutes or until firm. Roll heaped teaspoons of refrigerated mixture into balls; place on baking-paper-lined tray. Freeze until firm.

makes 12

2 eggs
2 egg yolks
⅓ cup (75g) caster sugar
85g dark eating chocolate, melted
1 cup (250ml) milk
1 cup (250ml) cream
1 cup (120g) almond meal
¼ cup (35g) plain flour
1 tablespoon cocoa powder
425g can seeded black cherries,
   drained
85g dark eating chocolate,
   grated coarsely

1 Preheat oven to 180°C/160°C fan-forced. Grease 23cm-square slab cake pan.
2 Beat eggs, egg yolks and sugar in medium bowl with electric mixer until combined; beat in cooled, melted chocolate. Slowly beat in milk and cream. Stir in almond meal, then sifted flour and cocoa.
3 Pour mixture into pan; sprinkle with cherries and grated chocolate.
4 Bake slice about 25 minutes. Stand slice 15 minutes; turn, top-side up, onto wire rack. Serve warm as a slice, or as a dessert with ice-cream or cream, if you like.

makes 20

black forest slice

chocolate plum brandy baskets

50g white chocolate Melts, melted
60g butter
⅓ cup (75g) firmly packed brown sugar
2 tablespoons golden syrup
⅓ cup (50g) plain flour
1 teaspoon cocoa powder
1 teaspoon ground ginger
5 drained whole canned plums (175g), seeded, quartered
white chocolate cream
½ cup (125ml) cream
180g white eating chocolate, chopped coarsely

1 Use white chocolate Melts to make curls (see page 112).
2 Make white chocolate cream.
3 Preheat oven to 180°C/160°C fan-forced. Grease two oven trays; line with baking paper.
4 Stir butter, sugar and syrup in small saucepan over low heat until smooth. Remove from heat; stir in sifted flour, cocoa and ginger.
5 Drop rounded teaspoons of mixture about 5cm apart onto trays. (Until you master the handling and baking time of the snaps, bake only two at a time.) Bake about 7 minutes or until brandy snaps bubble; cool on tray 30 seconds.

6 Using metal spatula, quickly lift brandy snap from tray; shape each brandy snap into a basket-shape around base of 3cm glass. Cool each brandy snap for about 1 minute; remove, place on wire rack to cool. Repeat with remaining mixture (see page 113).
7 Just before serving, fill baskets with white chocolate cream. Top with plum pieces and white chocolate curls.
white chocolate cream Stir cream and chocolate in small heatproof bowl over small saucepan of simmering water until smooth. Cool; refrigerate 30 minutes or until spreadable. Beat chocolate mixture in small bowl with electric mixer until firm peaks form.

makes 18

white chocolate and passionfruit mousse eggs

We used six 6-hole (1 tablespoon/20ml) easter egg moulds for this recipe. Or, make eggs in six batches. You will need about 3 passionfruit for this recipe.

300g white chocolate Melts, melted
100g white eating chocolate, chopped coarsely
20g unsalted butter
¼ cup (60ml) passionfruit pulp
1 egg, separated
⅔ cup (160ml) thickened cream, whipped

1 Using small paint brush, paint melted chocolate over inside of moulds (see page 113). Leave to set at room temperature. Gently remove eggs from moulds.
2 Meanwhile, stir chopped chocolate, butter and pulp in medium heatproof bowl over medium saucepan of simmering water until smooth. Stir in egg yolk. Cool.
3 Beat egg white in small bowl with electric mixer until soft peaks form. Fold egg white and cream into chocolate mixture, in two batches.
4 Divide mousse among eggs. Refrigerate 3 hours or overnight.
5 Serve drizzled with extra passionfruit pulp, if you like.

makes 36

chocolate fondants

These are the perfect do-ahead desserts; they can be frozen, ready-to-bake, weeks ahead. Make sure you're organised so the fondants are served and eaten while their centre is wonderfully soft and gooey.

200g dark eating chocolate, chopped coarsely
100g unsalted butter, chopped coarsely
1 tablespoon cocoa powder
1 tablespoon self-raising flour
⅓ cup (75g) caster sugar
3 eggs

1 Grease 6-hole (½ cup/125ml) friand pan evenly with a little melted butter.
2 Stir chocolate and butter in small heatproof bowl over small saucepan of simmering water until smooth.
3 Sift cocoa, flour and sugar into medium bowl; whisk in eggs and chocolate mixture.
4 Divide mixture among pan holes; cover pan with foil, freeze 3 hours or overnight.
5 Preheat oven to 220°C/200°C fan-forced.
6 Bake frozen fondants 7 minutes; turn pan, bake further 7 minutes. Stand fondants 2 minutes; loosen edges with knife, gently ease out of pan. Serve immediately with cream or ice-cream, if you like.

makes 6

Rose, violet, nasturtium and pansy petals are all edible and make beautiful additions to recipes.

⅓ cup (75g) caster sugar
¼ cup (42g) gelatine
750ml rosé wine
2 tablespoons cream
100g white eating chocolate, chopped coarsely
36 rose petals

rosé wine jellies

1 Sprinkle sugar and gelatine over 1 cup (250ml) of the wine in large heatproof jug; stand jug in medium saucepan of simmering water. Stir until gelatine dissolves.
2 Stir remaining wine into gelatine mixture. Pour mixture into two 18-hole (1 tablespoon/20ml) flexible jelly moulds. Refrigerate 3 hours or until firm.
3 Stir cream and chocolate in small heatproof bowl over small saucepan of simmering water until smooth. Refrigerate about 30 minutes, stirring occasionally, until spreadable.
4 Half-fill shallow baking dish with boiling water; stand jelly moulds in dish about 2 seconds or until jelly begins to come away from side of moulds. Carefully unmould jellies onto tray. Pipe or spoon chocolate mixture onto jellies; top with rose petals.

makes 36

100g unsalted butter, softened
½ cup (80g) icing sugar
½ cup (140g) crunchy
   peanut butter
12 5cm x 9cm ice-cream wafers
60g dark eating chocolate,
   melted
peanut praline
⅓ cup (45g) roasted unsalted
   peanuts
½ cup (110g) caster sugar
¼ cup (60ml) water

1 Make peanut praline.
2 Beat butter and sifted icing sugar in small bowl with electric mixer until light and fluffy; beat in peanut butter.
3 Spread half the peanut butter mixture over four wafers. Top each with another wafer; spread remaining peanut butter mixture over the top of each sandwich. Top with remaining wafers to make four triple-decker wafer sandwiches. Refrigerate 1 hour.
4 Using serrated knife, cut wafer sandwiches crossways into four. Dip tops of sandwiches into chocolate; sprinkle with praline. Refrigerate until set.

peanut praline Place nuts on baking-paper-lined oven tray. Stir sugar and the water in small saucepan over heat, without boiling, until sugar dissolves. Bring to the boil; boil, uncovered, without stirring, until golden brown. Pour mixture over nuts; leave to set at room temperature. Break brittle into small pieces.

makes 16

choc nut cream bites with peanut praline

frozen chocolate tiramisu bars

½ cup (125ml) coffee-flavoured
   liqueur
2 large chocolate muffins (230g),
   crumbled
500ml coffee ice-cream, softened
180g dark eating chocolate,
   melted
2 tablespoons cocoa powder

1 Line 6-hole (⅔ cup/160ml) loaf pan with foil, extending foil 5cm over sides.
2 Sprinkle liqueur over muffins in medium bowl; stir in ice-cream.
3 Divide ice-cream mixture among pan holes, cover with foil; freeze about 3 hours or until firm.
4 Remove ice-cream bars from pan; remove foil, place bars on tray. Freeze ice-cream bars until required.

5 Trace 12cm x 15cm rectangle on piece of paper. Cover paper with plastic wrap. Spread one-sixth of the chocolate onto plastic wrap into rectangle shape. Remove one ice-cream bar from the freezer; stand in centre of chocolate rectangle. Pull plastic wrap up to encase bottom and sides of ice-cream bar (see page 113); return to tray, freeze 1 minute or until chocolate sets. Gently peel away plastic wrap (see page 113); return ice-cream bar to tray, freeze. Repeat with remaining chocolate and ice-cream bars.
6 Dust tiramisu bars with sifted cocoa; serve with a shot of hot coffee, if you like.
tip If chocolate starts to thicken between wrapping ice-cream bars, re-melt.

makes 6

white chocolate, rhubarb and ginger trifles

You will need about four large stems of rhubarb for this recipe.

2 cups (220g) coarsely
  chopped rhubarb
2 tablespoons caster sugar
1 teaspoon finely grated
  orange rind
1 tablespoon orange juice
1 tablespoon finely chopped
  glacé ginger
12 gingernut biscuits (125g),
  chopped coarsely
1 cup (250ml) orange juice, extra
1 medium orange (240g),
  segmented (see page 114)
white chocolate cream
½ cup (125ml) cream
180g white eating chocolate,
  chopped coarsely

1 Make white chocolate cream.
2 Combine rhubarb, sugar, rind and juice in small saucepan; bring to the boil. Reduce heat; simmer, uncovered, stirring occasionally, about 5 minutes or until rhubarb softens. Cool; stir in ginger.
3 Divide rhubarb mixture among six ⅔ cup (160ml) glasses; top with combined biscuits and extra juice, then white chocolate cream and orange segments.
white chocolate cream Stir cream and chocolate in small heatproof bowl over small saucepan of simmering water until smooth. Refrigerate about 30 minutes or until spreadable. Beat chocolate mixture with electric mixer until firm peaks form.

serves 6

iced coconut slice

4 egg yolks
2 tablespoons caster sugar
100g white eating chocolate,
    melted
⅓ cup (80ml) coconut-flavoured
    liqueur
2 egg whites
300ml cream, whipped
1 small pineapple (900g), peeled,
    cored, chopped finely
½ cup finely shredded fresh mint
½ cup (125ml) pineapple juice

1 Line 14cm x 21cm loaf pan with strips of foil, extending foil 10cm over sides of pan.
2 Beat egg yolks and sugar in small bowl with electric mixer until thick and creamy; transfer mixture to large bowl. Stir in chocolate and liqueur.
3 Beat egg whites in small bowl with electric mixer until soft peaks form. Fold egg whites and cream into chocolate mixture, in two batches.
4 Pour mixture into pan; cover with foil, freeze overnight until firm.
5 Combine remaining ingredients in small bowl.
6 Serve pieces of slice topped with pineapple mixture.

serves 10

2 small apples (260g), peeled
4 sheets ready-rolled
  shortcrust pastry
⅓ cup (110g) chocolate
  hazelnut spread
1 egg white
1 tablespoon white sugar

1 Preheat oven to 190°C/170°C fan-forced. Grease two oven trays; line with baking paper.
2 Cut each apple into eight wedges; remove cores.
3 Cut 16 x 10cm rounds from pastry sheets. Drop rounded teaspoons of spread into centre of each round; top each with an apple wedge. Brush edges with a little egg white; fold rounds in half to enclose filling, pinch edges to seal. Place on trays.
4 Brush turnovers with remaining egg white; sprinkle with sugar. Bake about 20 minutes. Transfer to wire rack to cool.

makes 16

choc-nut apple turnovers

2 medium pears (460g), peeled,
  cored, chopped finely
25g dark eating chocolate,
  chopped coarsely
mocha crumble
1 teaspoon instant coffee granules
½ teaspoon hot water
¼ cup (35g) plain flour
1 tablespoon self-raising flour
2 tablespoons raw sugar
35g unsalted butter, chopped
2 teaspoons cocoa powder

1 Make mocha crumble.
2 Preheat oven to 200°C/180°C
fan-forced. Grease six ⅓ cup (80ml)
ovenproof dishes; place on oven tray.
3 Divide pear and chocolate
among dishes; coarsely grate
crumble over pear mixture.
4 Bake about 20 minutes. Stand
5 minutes before serving with
cream or ice-cream, if you like.
mocha crumble Dissolve coffee
in the water in processor. Add
remaining ingredients; process
until combined. Wrap in plastic
wrap; freeze about 1 hour or
until firm.

serves 6

mocha pear crumble

pikelets with raspberry butter

1 cup (150g) self-raising flour
2 tablespoons cocoa powder
¼ cup (55g) caster sugar
1 egg
1¼ cups (310ml) buttermilk
raspberry butter
1 cup (150g) frozen raspberries,
    thawed
150g unsalted butter, softened
⅔ cup (110g) icing sugar

1 Make raspberry butter.
2 Sift flour, cocoa and sugar
into small bowl; whisk in egg
and buttermilk.
3 Heat greased large heavy-based
frying pan; drop tablespoons of
batter into pan. Cook pikelets
until bubbles appear on surface;
turn pikelets with metal spatula to
brown the other side.
4 Serve pikelets warm with
raspberry butter and fresh
raspberries, if you like.
raspberry butter Push raspberries
through fine sieve into small bowl;
discard seeds. Beat butter and
sifted icing sugar in small bowl with
electric mixer until light and fluffy.
Beat in raspberry puree.

serves 6

chocomarmalaska

4 large chocolate muffins (460g)
⅓ cup (115g) orange marmalade
250ml chocolate ice-cream
3 egg whites
¾ cup (165g) firmly packed
  brown sugar
1 teaspoon finely grated
  orange rind

1 Cut tops off muffins; discard. Hollow out muffin centres, leaving a 1cm border.
2 Drop level tablespoons of marmalade into each muffin. Top with ice-cream. Stand muffins on oven tray, freeze about 1 hour or until firm.
3 Preheat oven to 240°C/220°C fan-forced.
4 Just before serving, beat egg whites in small bowl with electric mixer until soft peaks form; gradually add sugar, beating until dissolved between additions. Beat in rind.
5 Spread meringue over muffins. Bake about 2 minutes or until browned lightly. Serve immediately.

serves 4

chocolate pistachio tart

½ cup (70g) roasted unsalted pistachios
100g unsalted butter, softened
½ cup (110g) caster sugar
2 eggs
⅔ cup (100g) self-raising flour
⅓ cup (35g) cocoa powder
½ cup (160g) raspberry jam
12 roasted unsalted pistachios, extra
40g dark chocolate Melts, melted

pastry
1¼ cups (185g) plain flour
½ cup (80g) icing sugar
125g cold unsalted butter, chopped coarsely
2 tablespoons iced water, approximately

1 Make pastry.
2 Grease 12.5cm x 35cm (or 22cm round) loose-based fluted flan tin. Reserve one-quarter of the dough for decoration. Roll remaining dough between sheets of baking paper until large enough to line tin. Ease dough into tin; press into base and sides. Trim edges; prick base all over with fork. Refrigerate 30 minutes.
3 Roll out reserved dough on floured surface, cut out 12 x 2cm rounds from reserved dough; place on baking-paper-lined tray. Refrigerate 30 minutes.
4 Preheat oven to 200°C/180°C fan-forced.
5 Blend or process nuts finely.

6 Beat butter and sugar in small bowl with electric mixer until light and fluffy. Beat in eggs, one at a time. Transfer mixture to medium bowl; stir in sifted flour and cocoa, and nuts. Spread jam over base of pastry case; top with pistachio filling. Top filling with pastry rounds. Bake 15 minutes.
7 Reduce oven to 180°C/160°C fan-forced; bake 25 minutes. Cool.
8 Dip extra nuts in chocolate; place on pastry rounds. Cool before slicing.

pastry Process sifted flour and sugar with butter until crumbly. Add enough of the water until ingredients just come together when processed. Knead dough on floured surface until smooth. Cover; refrigerate 30 minutes.

serves 16

We used six 6-hole (1 tablespoon/20ml) easter egg moulds for this recipe. Or, make eggs in six batches.

300g dark chocolate Melts, melted
1 cup (160g) coarsely chopped raisins
⅓ cup (80ml) dark rum
100g milk eating chocolate, chopped coarsely
20g unsalted butter
1 egg, separated
⅔ cup (160ml) thickened cream, whipped

1 Using small paint brush, paint dark chocolate over inside of moulds (see page 113). Leave to set at room temperature. Gently remove eggs from mould.
2 Combine raisins and half of the rum in small bowl.
3 Stir milk chocolate, butter and remaining rum in medium heatproof bowl over medium saucepan of simmering water until smooth. Stir in egg yolk; cool.
4 Beat egg white in small bowl with electric mixer until soft peaks form. Fold egg white and cream into chocolate mixture, in two batches.
5 Divide raisin mixture among chocolate eggs; top with mousse. Refrigerate 3 hours or overnight.
6 Serve with dark chocolate curls (see page 112), if you like.

makes 36

rum and raisin chocolate mousse eggs

opera gateau

Use a hot, dry knife, to trim edges from cake before slicing.

4 eggs
1¼ cups (150g) almond meal
1 cup (160g) icing sugar
⅓ cup (50g) plain flour
25g unsalted butter, melted
4 egg whites
1 tablespoon caster sugar
coffee butter cream
¼ cup (60ml) milk
¼ cup (55g) brown sugar
2 teaspoons instant
    coffee granules
1 egg yolk
125g unsalted butter, softened
coffee syrup
⅓ cup (80ml) boiling water
2 tablespoons caster sugar
1 tablespoon instant
    coffee granules
ganache
160g dark eating chocolate,
    chopped coarsely
⅓ cup (80ml) cream
glaze
50g unsalted butter
75g dark eating chocolate

1 Preheat oven to 220°C/200°C fan-forced. Grease two 25cm x 30cm swiss roll pans; line bases with baking paper, extending paper 5cm over long sides.
2 Beat eggs, almond meal and sifted icing sugar in small bowl with electric mixer until creamy; beat in flour. Transfer mixture to large bowl; stir in butter.
3 Beat egg whites in small bowl with electric mixer until soft peaks form; add caster sugar, beating until sugar dissolves. Fold into almond mixture, in two batches.
4 Divide mixture between pans. Bake about 7 minutes. Cool.
5 Make coffee butter cream, coffee syrup and ganache.
6 Cut each cake into a 20cm x 25cm rectangle and a 10cm x 25cm rectangle (see page 114).
7 Place one of the large cake rectangles on baking-paper-lined tray; brush with half of the coffee syrup. Spread cake with half of the butter cream; refrigerate 10 minutes. Top butter cream with the two small cake rectangles, side-by-side. Brush with the remaining coffee syrup; spread with ganache. Top with remaining cake; refrigerate 10 minutes. Spread top of cake with remaining butter cream; refrigerate 3 hours (see page 114).

8 Meanwhile, make glaze.
9 Working quickly, spread glaze evenly over cake. Refrigerate 30 minutes or until glaze has set.
coffee butter cream Stir milk, sugar and coffee in small saucepan, over low heat, until sugar dissolves. Whisk egg yolk in small bowl; gradually whisk in hot milk mixture. Return custard to pan; stir over heat, without boiling, about 5 minutes or until thickened slightly. Cool. Beat butter in small bowl with electric mixer until light and fluffy; beat in custard.
coffee syrup Stir ingredients in small bowl.
ganache Stir ingredients in small heatproof bowl over small saucepan of simmering water until smooth. Refrigerate until spreadable.
glaze Stir ingredients in small heatproof bowl over small saucepan of simmering water until smooth. Use while warm.

serves 24

250g dark eating chocolate, melted
1¼ cups (135g) coarsely chopped roasted walnuts
150g dark eating chocolate, chopped coarsely
¾ cup (165g) firmly packed brown sugar
3 eggs

1 Grease 19cm x 29cm slice pan; line base and sides with foil, extending foil 5cm over long sides.
2 Spread melted chocolate over base of pan; refrigerate until set.
3 Preheat oven to 180°C/160°C fan-forced.
4 Process nuts, chopped chocolate, sugar and eggs until combined. Pour nut mixture over chocolate base. Bake about 20 minutes. Cool.
5 Remove from pan; carefully remove foil. Cut into squares.

makes 24

decadent double-choc slice

white chocolate lamingtons

6 eggs
⅔ cup (150g) caster sugar
80g white eating chocolate, chopped finely
½ cup (75g) plain flour
⅓ cup (50g) self-raising flour
⅓ cup (50g) cornflour
4 cups (640g) icing sugar
¾ cup (180ml) milk
2 cups (150g) shredded coconut
100g white eating chocolate, grated finely

1 Preheat oven to 180°C/160°C fan-forced. Grease 23cm-square slab cake pan; line base and sides with baking paper, extending paper 5cm over sides.
2 Beat eggs in medium bowl with electric mixer about 10 minutes or until thick and creamy; gradually beat in caster sugar, dissolving between each addition. Fold in chopped chocolate and triple-sifted flours.
3 Spread mixture into pan; bake about 35 minutes. Turn cake immediately onto baking-paper-lined wire rack to cool; refrigerate while preparing the icing.

4 Sift icing sugar into medium heatproof bowl; stir in milk. Place bowl over medium saucepan of simmering water, stir until icing is of a coating consistency.
5 Cut cold cake into 25 squares.
6 Dip each square of cake into icing, drain off excess. Toss squares in combined coconut and grated chocolate. Place lamingtons on wire rack to set.

makes 25

mini choc-chip banana loaves

1 cup (460g) mashed overripe
  banana
¾ cup (165g) firmly packed
  brown sugar
2 eggs
60g butter, melted
¼ cup (60ml) buttermilk
⅔ cup (100g) self-raising flour
⅔ cup (100g) wholemeal
  self-raising flour
½ cup (95g) milk Choc Bits

1 Preheat oven to 180°C/160°C
fan-forced. Grease 8-hole (¾ cup/
180ml) mini loaf pan; line base and
two short sides with baking paper.
2 Combine banana and sugar in
large bowl; stir in eggs, butter and
buttermilk, then sifted flours and
Choc Bits.
3 Divide mixture among pan holes;
bake about 20 minutes. Stand
loaves 5 minutes; turn, top-side up,
onto wire rack to cool. Serve warm
with butter, if you like.

makes 8

black forest chocolate boxes

2 tablespoons cocoa powder
2 tablespoons water
70g dark eating chocolate, melted
70g butter, melted
⅔ cup (150g) firmly packed
   brown sugar
½ cup (60g) almond meal
2 eggs, separated
200g dark eating chocolate,
   melted, extra
425g can seeded black cherries
1 teaspoon cornflour
1 tablespoon kirsch
⅓ cup (110g) cherry jam,
   warmed, sieved
kirsch cream
250g mascarpone cheese
2 tablespoons icing sugar
1 tablespoon kirsch

1 Preheat oven to 160°C/140°C fan-forced. Grease deep 23cm-square cake pan; line with baking paper, extending paper 5cm over sides.

2 Blend sifted cocoa with the water in large bowl until smooth. Stir in chocolate, butter, sugar, almond meal and egg yolks.

3 Beat egg whites in small bowl with electric mixer until soft peaks form; fold into chocolate mixture.

4 Pour mixture into pan; bake about 40 minutes. Stand cake 10 minutes; turn, top-side up, onto wire rack to cool.

5 Trim cake to 20cm square. Cover; freeze cake 30 minutes or until firm. Cut cake into 16 x 5cm squares.

6 Line a flat tray with baking paper. Spread extra chocolate into 32cm square; set at room temperature. Cut chocolate to 30cm square; cut square into 36 x 5cm squares, then cut each square in half to give 72 rectangles. Refrigerate 10 minutes.

7 Drain cherries; reserve syrup. Blend cornflour with 1 tablespoon of the syrup in small saucepan. Stir in remaining syrup and liqueur; cook, stirring, until mixture boils and thickens. Reduce heat; simmer cherry glaze, stirring, 1 minute. Cool.

8 Make kirsch cream.

9 Brush edges of cake squares with jam; press chocolate rectangles onto sides of cakes (see page 114). Spoon kirsch cream into centre of cakes; top with cherries and cherry glaze.

kirsch cream Combine ingredients in small bowl.

makes 16

90g white eating chocolate, chopped coarsely
90g unsalted butter, chopped coarsely
½ cup (110g) firmly packed brown sugar
2 tablespoons golden syrup
½ cup (125ml) milk
¾ cup (110g) plain flour
¼ cup (35g) self-raising flour
1 egg
2 tablespoons milk Choc Bits
1 tablespoon icing sugar

1 Preheat oven to 160°C/140°C fan-forced. Grease 9-hole (½ cup/125ml) friand pan; line bases with baking paper.
2 Stir chocolate, butter, brown sugar, syrup and milk in medium saucepan, over low heat, until smooth. Cool 15 minutes.
3 Whisk in sifted flours and egg. Stir in Choc Bits. Divide mixture among pan holes.
4 Bake cakes about 25 minutes. Stand cakes 5 minutes; turn, top-side up, onto wire rack to cool. Serve dusted with sifted icing sugar.

makes 9

caramel choc-chip mud cakes

180g white eating chocolate,
  melted
1¼ cups (95g) shredded coconut
silver cachous

1 Line two trays with baking paper.
2 Combine chocolate and coconut in medium bowl. Drop heaped tablespoons of mixture onto trays; shape mixture into wreaths using the end of a wooden spoon to make holes in the centre of each wreath.
3 Decorate wreaths with cachous. Refrigerate until set. Tie with ribbon, if you like.

makes 8

coconut christmas wreaths

white chocolate and raspberry mille-feuilles

1 sheet ready-rolled puff pastry
50g white eating chocolate, melted
1 tablespoon raspberry jam
½ cup (125ml) thickened cream
50g white eating chocolate, grated finely
60g fresh raspberries
30g white eating chocolate, chopped coarsely
1 tablespoon thickened cream, extra
1 tablespoon icing sugar

1 Preheat oven to 240°C/220°C fan-forced. Grease oven tray.
2 Place pastry sheet on tray; place a second oven tray on top. Bake about 15 minutes or until pastry is browned and crisp. Cool 2 minutes.
3 Spread pastry sheet with melted chocolate, then jam. Cut into 18 rectangles.
4 Beat cream in small bowl with electric mixer until firm peaks form; fold in grated chocolate.
5 Spread cream mixture over jam; sandwich pastry rectangles with raspberries.
6 Stir chopped chocolate and extra cream in small heatproof bowl over small saucepan of simmering water until smooth.
7 Drizzle mille-feuilles with chocolate mixture; dust with sifted icing sugar.

makes 9

lime and pineapple loaves

100g unsalted butter, softened
1 tablespoon finely grated
   lime rind
½ cup (110g) caster sugar
2 eggs
¾ cup (110g) self-raising flour
2 tablespoons milk
½ small pineapple (450g), peeled,
   cored, sliced thinly
lime ganache
180g white eating chocolate,
   chopped coarsely
2 tablespoons lime juice
¼ cup (60ml) cream

1 Preheat oven to 150°C/130°C fan-forced. Grease 8-hole (¾ cup/ 180ml) mini loaf pan; line bases with baking paper.
2 Beat butter, rind, sugar, eggs, flour and milk in medium bowl with electric mixer, on low speed, until combined. Increase speed to medium; beat about 3 minutes or until mixture is light and fluffy. Divide mixture among pan holes; cover pan loosely with foil. Bake about 25 minutes. Stand cakes 5 minutes; turn, top-side up, onto wire rack to cool.
3 Meanwhile, make lime ganache.
4 Split loaves in half. Sandwich loaves with half of the ganache and half of the pineapple. Top loaves with remaining ganache and pineapple.

lime ganache Stir chocolate, juice and cream in small heatproof bowl over small saucepan of simmering water until smooth. Refrigerate until spreadable.

makes 8

white choc-chip orange and cranberry mini muffins

2 cups (300g) self-raising flour
½ cup (110g) caster sugar
¾ cup (135g) white Choc Bits
½ cup (65g) dried cranberries
60g butter, melted
¾ cup (180ml) milk
1 egg
2 teaspoons finely grated
   orange rind
¼ cup (60ml) orange juice
cranberry icing
1½ cups (240g) icing sugar
½ teaspoon vegetable oil
2 tablespoons cranberry juice,
   approximately

1 Preheat oven to 200°C/180°C fan-forced. Line four 12-hole (1 tablespoon/20ml) mini muffin pans with paper cases.
2 Sift dry ingredients into medium bowl; stir in remaining ingredients.
3 Divide mixture among cases. Bake about 10 minutes. Stand muffins 2 minutes; turn, top-side up, onto wire rack to cool.
4 Meanwhile, make cranberry icing. Spread muffins with icing.
cranberry icing Sift icing sugar into small heatproof bowl. Stir in oil and enough juice to make a paste. Stir over small saucepan of simmering water until icing is spreadable.

makes 48

milk chocolate custard tarts

⅓ cup (75g) caster sugar
2 tablespoons cornflour
300ml cream
100g milk eating chocolate,
  chopped coarsely
4 egg yolks
1 sheet ready-rolled butter
  puff pastry
1 tablespoon icing sugar

1 Preheat oven to 220°C/200°C
fan-forced. Grease two 12-hole
(1 tablespoon/20ml) mini muffin pans.
2 Combine caster sugar and
cornflour in small saucepan; stir in
cream. Cook, stirring, until mixture
boils and thickens. Reduce heat;
simmer, stirring, 1 minute. Remove
pan from heat. Add chocolate and
egg yolks; stir until smooth.
3 Cut pastry sheet in half; stack
pastry halves on top of each other.
Roll pastry up tightly from short
side; cut into 24 x 5mm-thick slices.
4 Roll slices between sheets of
baking paper into 8cm rounds;
press rounds into pan holes.
5 Divide custard among pastry
cases. Bake about 10 minutes.
Stand tarts 5 minutes; serve warm
tarts dusted with sifted icing sugar.

makes 24

mocha cream hearts

50g unsalted butter
½ cup (125ml) water
½ cup (75g) plain flour
2 teaspoons cocoa powder
2 eggs
150g milk eating chocolate,
    melted
mocha cream
2 teaspoons instant
    coffee granules
1 teaspoon hot water
300ml thickened cream
¼ cup (40g) icing sugar

1 Preheat oven to 200°C/180°C fan-forced. Grease oven tray. Trace 8 x 7cm hearts onto a piece of baking paper to use as a guide; line tray with paper.
2 Combine butter and the water in medium saucepan; bring to the boil. Add sifted flour and cocoa; beat with wooden spoon over high heat until mixture comes away from base and side of pan to form a smooth ball. Transfer mixture to small bowl; beat in eggs, one at a time, with electric mixer until mixture becomes glossy.
3 Spoon mixture into piping bag fitted with a 5mm plain tube. Pipe half of the mixture into eight hearts on tray, using paper as a guide. Pipe remaining mixture directly on top of previous hearts. (See page 115.)
4 Bake hearts 7 minutes.

5 Reduce oven to180°C/160°C fan-forced; bake hearts about 10 minutes or until crisp. Remove from oven. Using serrated knife, split hearts in half, return to trays. Bake about 10 minutes or until dried out.
6 Meanwhile, make mocha cream.
7 Place half of the hearts, top-side up, on a wire rack over tray; spread with chocolate. Leave to set at room temperature. (See page 115.)
8 Fill remaining hearts with mocha cream; top with chocolate coated hearts. (See page 115.)
mocha cream Dissolve coffee in the water; cool. Beat cream, sifted icing sugar and coffee mixture in small bowl with electric mixer until firm peaks form.

makes 8

1 tablespoon anise seeds
200g dark eating chocolate,
  melted
¾ cup (120g) finely chopped
  dried pears
½ cup (65g) finely chopped
  roasted macadamias

1 Dry-fry anise in small frying pan until fragrant; chop finely.
2 Warm a tray on stove top or in oven; cover with baking paper.
3 Combine anise with remaining ingredients in medium bowl.
4 Spread chocolate mixture onto tray as thinly as possible; refrigerate until set.
5 Break bark into rough pieces. Serve with coffee or ice-cream, if you like.

spicy fruit and nut bark

cinnamon prune swirls

1 seeded prune, chopped finely
1 tablespoon chocolate-flavoured
  liqueur
20 x 3cm milk chocolate pastilles
whipped cinnamon ganache
100g milk eating chocolate,
  chopped coarsely
2 tablespoons cream
¼ teaspoon ground cinnamon

1 Make whipped cinnamon ganache.
2 Meanwhile, combine prune and liqueur in small saucepan; stir over low heat until the liqueur has been absorbed. Cool.
3 Spoon ganache into piping bag fitted with small fluted tube. Pipe swirls of ganache onto pastilles; top with a piece of prune.

whipped cinnamon ganache
Stir chocolate, cream and cinnamon in small heatproof bowl over small saucepan of simmering water until smooth. Remove from heat; cool. Beat chocolate mixture in small bowl with electric mixer until spreadable.

makes 20

milk chocolate praline eggs

We used Kinder Surprise chocolate eggs available in most supermarkets.

12 x 20g hollow chocolate eggs
200g milk eating chocolate,
 chopped coarsely
½ cup (125ml) cream
praline
⅓ cup (45g) coarsely chopped
 roasted hazelnuts
⅓ cup (55g) coarsely chopped
 roasted almonds
½ cup (110g) caster sugar
2 tablespoons water

1 Make praline.
2 Carefully cut tops from chocolate eggs; discard tops.
3 Stir chocolate and cream in small heatproof bowl over small saucepan of simmering water until smooth; cool. Stir praline into chocolate mixture. Refrigerate until spreadable.
4 Place chocolate eggs, cut-side up, in egg cups. Spoon chocolate praline mixture into eggs.
praline Place nuts on baking-paper-lined oven tray. Combine sugar and the water in small saucepan; stir over heat, without boiling, until sugar dissolves. Bring to the boil; boil, uncovered, until toffee is golden brown. Pour toffee over nuts; leave to set at room temperature. Break praline into pieces; process until chopped finely.

makes 12

⅓ cup (75g) caster sugar
2 tablespoons water
⅔ cup (160ml) cream
200g dark eating chocolate,
  chopped coarsely
1 teaspoon sea salt flakes
200g milk eating chocolate,
  melted

salted caramel truffles

1 Combine sugar and the water in small saucepan; stir over heat, without boiling, until sugar dissolves. Bring to the boil; boil, uncovered, without stirring, until golden brown. Add cream; stir over low heat until toffee pieces melt. Remove from heat; stir in dark chocolate and half of the salt until smooth. Refrigerate mixture overnight.
2 Working with a quarter of the chocolate mixture at a time (keep remainder refrigerated), roll rounded teaspoons of mixture into balls; place on foil-lined tray. Freeze until firm.
3 Working quickly, using two forks, dip truffles in milk chocolate (see page 115). Return truffles to tray; sprinkle with remaining salt. Refrigerate truffles until firm.

makes 25

2 eggs, separated
1 tablespoon caster sugar
50g dark eating chocolate, melted
2 tablespoons mint-flavoured liqueur
⅔ cup (160ml) cream
8 paddle-pop sticks

1 Beat egg yolks and sugar in small bowl with electric mixer until thick and creamy; beat in chocolate and liqueur. Transfer to medium bowl.
2 Beat cream in small bowl with electric mixer until soft peaks form; fold into chocolate mixture.
3 Beat egg whites in small bowl with electric mixer until soft peaks form; fold into chocolate mixture.
4 Pour mixture into eight ¼ cup (60ml) ice-block moulds; push paddle-pop sticks into centre of each mould. Press lids on firmly; freeze overnight.

after dinner mint ices

makes 8

dark chocolate pistachio brittle

2 cups (440g) caster sugar
½ cup (125ml) water
1 cup (140g) roasted pistachios,
   chopped coarsely
200g dark eating chocolate,
   melted

1 Line oven tray with baking paper.
2 Combine sugar and the water in medium saucepan; stir over heat, without boiling, until sugar dissolves. Bring to the boil; boil, uncovered, without stirring, until golden brown. Allow bubbles to subside; add nuts. Pour mixture onto tray; leave to set at room temperature.
3 Spread chocolate over brittle; refrigerate about 10 minutes or until chocolate sets. Break brittle into pieces.

serves 15

chocolate, lemon and thyme truffles

250g white eating chocolate, chopped coarsely
¼ cup (60ml) cream
1 teaspoon finely grated lemon rind
1 tablespoon lemon juice
½ teaspoon finely chopped fresh thyme leaves
250g white eating chocolate, melted
2 teaspoons finely grated lemon rind, extra

1 Stir chopped chocolate, cream, rind and juice in small heatproof bowl over small saucepan of simmering water until smooth. Remove from heat; stir in thyme. Refrigerate mixture overnight.
2 Working with a quarter of the chocolate mixture at a time (keep remainder refrigerated), roll rounded teaspoons of mixture into balls; place on foil-lined tray. Freeze until firm.
3 Working quickly, using two forks, dip truffles in melted chocolate (see page 115). Return truffles to tray; sprinkle with extra rind. Refrigerate truffles until firm.

makes 25

milk chocolate beetroot cake

3 small beetroot (300g), peeled
250g butter, softened
1 cup (220g) caster sugar
4 eggs
1 cup (150g) plain flour
1 cup (150g) self-raising flour
¼ cup (25g) cocoa powder
100g milk eating chocolate,
　chopped coarsely
fluffy chocolate ganache
200g dark eating chocolate,
　chopped coarsely
½ cup (125ml) cream

1 Preheat oven to 170°C/150°C fan-forced. Grease 20cm x 30cm lamington pan; line with baking paper, extending paper 5cm over long sides.
2 Grate beetroot coarsely.
3 Beat butter and sugar in small bowl with electric mixer until light and fluffy. Beat in eggs, one at a time. Stir in sifted flours and cocoa, then chocolate and beetroot.
4 Spread mixture into pan; bake about 40 minutes. Stand cake 5 minutes; turn, top-side up, onto wire rack to cool.
5 Meanwhile, make fluffy chocolate ganache.
6 Spread cake with ganache.
fluffy chocolate ganache
Stir ingredients in small heatproof bowl over small saucepan of simmering water until smooth; cool. Refrigerate until spreadable.

serves 20

50g dark eating chocolate,
  chopped coarsely
2 tablespoons raspberry-flavoured
  liqueur
1 medium pear (230g),
  chopped finely
125ml vanilla ice-cream

1 Stir chocolate and liqueur in small heatproof bowl over small saucepan of simmering water until smooth.
2 Divide half of the chocolate mixture among six 1/3 cup (80ml) glasses. Top with half of the pear, half of the ice-cream and remaining chocolate mixture. Top with remaining ice-cream and pear.

serves 6

chocolate and pear shots

praline rocky road ice-cream

500ml chocolate ice-cream, softened
½ cup (125g) coarsely chopped glacé peaches
¾ cup (90g) coarsely chopped roasted pecans
coconut praline
⅔ cup (150g) caster sugar
2 tablespoons water
½ cup (40g) toasted shredded coconut

1 Combine ice-cream, peaches and nuts in large bowl. Freeze until almost firm.
2 Meanwhile, make coconut praline.
3 Stir praline through ice-cream mixture. Spread mixture into 15cm x 25cm loaf pan, cover with foil; freeze until firm.
4 Serve scoops of ice-cream sprinkled with dark chocolate curls (see page 112), if you like.
coconut praline Line oven tray with baking paper. Combine sugar and the water in medium saucepan; stir over heat, without boiling, until sugar dissolves. Bring to the boil; boil, uncovered, without stirring, until golden brown. Stir in coconut. Pour mixture onto tray; set at room temperature. Chop coarsely.

serves 4

crunchy bubble bars

4 cups (180g) coco pops
250g dark eating chocolate,
  chopped coarsely
100g butter, chopped coarsely
¼ cup (60ml) light corn syrup

1 Grease 20cm x 30cm lamington
pan; line with baking paper,
extending paper 5cm over
long sides.
2 Process half of the coco pops
until coarse.
3 Stir chocolate, butter and syrup
in large heatproof bowl over large
saucepan of simmering water until
smooth. Remove from heat; stir in
all coco pops.
4 Spread mixture into pan;
refrigerate until set. Cut into bars.

makes 40

raspberry rapture ice-cream cakes

500ml raspberry ice-cream,
  softened
180g white eating chocolate,
  melted
pink food colouring
450g madeira cake
¼ cup (80g) raspberry jam

1 Grease 15cm x 25cm loaf pan;
line with baking paper, extending
paper 5cm over long sides.
2 Spread ice-cream into pan,
cover with foil; freeze until firm.
3 Remove ice-cream from pan. Cut
six 6.5cm hearts from ice-cream;
place hearts on baking-paper-lined
tray, cover with foil; freeze until firm.
4 Line another tray with baking
paper. Tint melted chocolate
pink with food colouring. Spread
chocolate into 22cm x 30cm
rectangle on tray; stand at room
temperature about 5 minutes or
until almost set. Cut 12 x 6.5cm
hearts from chocolate (see page
115). Return to tray; refrigerate
until set.

5 Meanwhile, freeze cake until
firm. Slice cake into 12 x 1cm-thick
slices. Cut one 6.5cm heart from
each slice.
6 Spread one side of all cakes
with jam; top with chocolate
hearts. Sandwich plain sides of
cakes with ice-cream hearts. Serve
immediately or return to freezer
until required.

makes 6

coconut rough trio

100g milk eating chocolate, melted
1½ cups (115g) toasted shredded coconut
100g white eating chocolate, melted
100g dark eating chocolate, melted

1 Grease 8cm x 26cm bar pan; line with baking paper, extending paper 5cm over long sides.
2 Combine milk chocolate and ½ cup of the coconut in small bowl; spread mixture into pan. Refrigerate about 5 minutes or until firm.
3 Combine white chocolate and half of the remaining coconut in small bowl; spread mixture over milk chocolate base. Refrigerate about 5 minutes or until firm.
4 Combine dark chocolate and remaining coconut in small bowl; spread over white chocolate. Refrigerate about 30 minutes or until firm.
5 Remove from pan; stand 5 minutes before slicing with a hot, dry knife.

makes 25

23cm-square slab cake pan

26cm x 32cm swiss roll pan

8-hole (³⁄₄ cup/180ml) mini loaf pan

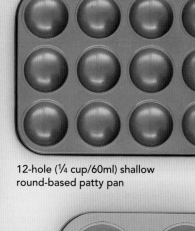

12-hole (¼ cup/60ml) shallow
round-based patty pan

6-hole (¹⁄₃ cup/80ml) friand pan

cutters

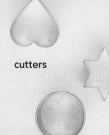

8cm x
26cm
bar cake
pan

19cm x 29cm slice pan

6-hole (³⁄₄ cup/180ml)
texas muffin pan

14cm x 21cm loaf pan

9-hole (¹⁄₃ cup/80ml) friand pan

12-hole (1 tablespoon/20ml)
mini muffin pan

equipment

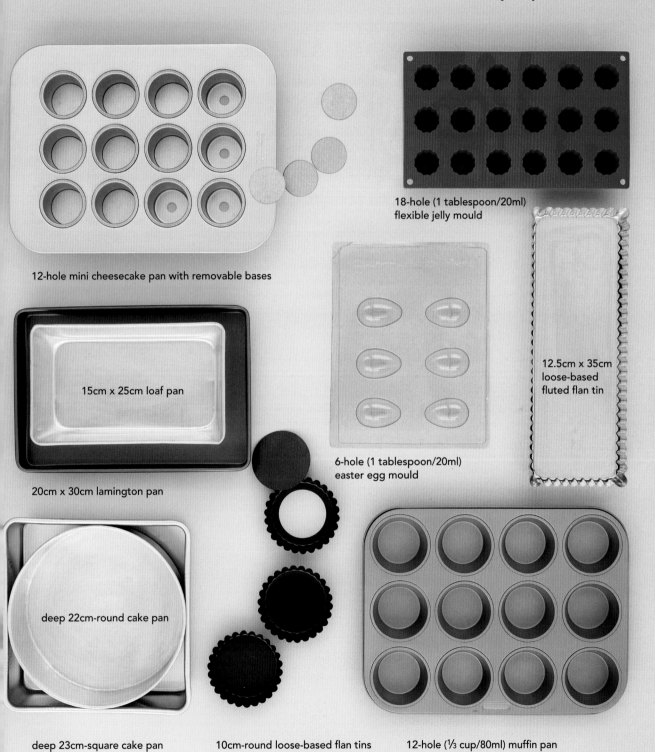

12-hole mini cheesecake pan with removable bases

18-hole (1 tablespoon/20ml)
flexible jelly mould

15cm x 25cm loaf pan

20cm x 30cm lamington pan

6-hole (1 tablespoon/20ml)
easter egg mould

12.5cm x 35cm
loose-based
fluted flan tin

deep 22cm-round cake pan

deep 23cm-square cake pan

10cm-round loose-based flan tins

12-hole (⅓ cup/80ml) muffin pan

Cooling chocolate hazelnut thins

As soon as the thins are baked, remove them from the oven; quickly slide a metal spatula under each thin to loosen them. Quickly place each warm thin over a rolling pin to cool completely.

Piping churros into oil

Spoon churros mixture into fabric piping bag fitted with a 1.5cm fluted tube. Once oil has reached correct deep-frying temperature (between 180°C and 190°C), hold piping as close to the oil as possible. Carefully pipe 7cm lengths of batter into oil, using a knife or metal spatula to cut lengths.

Melting chocolate

Place chocolate in a small heatproof bowl over a small saucepan of simmering water. Do not allow the water to touch the bottom of the bowl. Stir the chocolate until smooth, then immediately remove the bowl from the pan. Do not allow any water to come in contact with the chocolate or it will sieze.

Making chocolate curls

Spread melted chocolate evenly over a cold surface, such as marble or a flat oven tray; leave at room temperature until almost set. Drag the blade of a large sharp knife, held at about a 45° angle, across the chocolate, to make curls. It is important that chocolate is at the right stage. If chocolate is not set enough, it will not curl and if the chocolate is set too much the curls will break. Another way to make simple chocolate curls is to scrape along the side of a block of chocolate with a vegetable peeler.

tips & techniques

Painting easter egg moulds with chocolate

Use clean, dry plastic easter egg moulds (see page 111) which are available from specialty cookware shops. Using a small artist's brush dipped in melted chocolate, brush a thick, even layer of chocolate inside moulds; set at room temperature. To remove eggs, carefully invert mould onto board and gently tap eggs with finger until the eggs release from the mould.

Shaping brandy snap baskets

Once snaps begin to bubble, remove from oven and stand on trays about 1 minute or until firm enough to lift, but still flexible. Working quickly, slide a metal spatula under each snap to loosen them. Quickly lift one snap from oven tray and shape around base of 3cm glass. Cool about 1 minute or until firm, then transfer to wire rack to cool completely. If remaining snaps become too firm to handle, return tray to oven for a minute to re-soften.

Wrapping frozen chocolate tiramisu bars in chocolate

Trace a 12cm x 15cm rectangle on a piece of paper to use as a guide. Place a sheet of plastic wrap over paper. Spread chocolate over plastic wrap, into rectangle shape, using guide. Working quickly, place one ice-cream bar in centre of chocolate rectangle; lift corners and sides of plastic wrap above ice-cream bar to encase bottom and sides in chocolate. Place on a tray and freeze until chocolate sets.

Unwrapping frozen chocolate tiramisu bars

Once the chocolate has set, working with one bar at a time (keep remaining bars in freezer), carefully peel the plastic wrap away from the chocolate. Serve tiramisu bars immediately dusted with sifted cocoa powder or return to freezer until required.

Cutting & layering opera gateau

Cut each cake into a 20cm x 25cm rectangle and a 10cm x 25cm rectangle. Using a pastry brush, brush one of the large rectangles with half of the coffee syrup, then spread with half of the buttercream. Place the two small rectangles, side-by-side, on top of the buttercream, ensuring all edges and corners are aligned. Brush cakes with the remaining coffee syrup, then spread with the ganache.

Finishing opera gateau

Place the remaining large rectangle on top of ganache, then spread with the remaining buttercream. Refrigerate about 3 hours or until buttercream is firm. Working quickly, spread the glaze evenly over cake, then refrigerate until glaze has set. Glaze must be used while still warm, for a glossy finish to the top of your cake. Use a hot, dry knife to trim any uneven edges before slicing to serve.

Segmenting oranges

Cut a slice off the top and bottom of the orange; stand orange upright and cut all around, just inside pith, to remove peel. Cutting towards the centre, cut down each side of each membrane to form wedges or segments. Segment oranges over a small bowl to catch the juice.

Assembling black forest chocolate boxes

Spread chocolate onto baking-paper-lined tray into a 32cm square and allow to set at room temperature. Trim chocolate to a 30cm square, then cut square into 36 x 5cm squares. Cut each square in half to give 72 x 2.5cm x 5cm rectangles. Spread the sides of each cake with a little warmed and sieved jam. Carefully press chocolate rectangles onto sides of cakes, ensuring all corners are aligned, to create chocolate boxes.

Piping mocha cream hearts

Trace eight 7cm hearts on a piece of baking paper; place on a greased oven tray. Spoon the choux mixture into a piping bag fitted with a 5mm plain tube. Pipe half of the mixture onto paper, tracing outlines of hearts, then filling centres. Pipe the remaining mixture directly on top of the first hearts. You will have eight double-layered hearts. Bake hearts until crisp, then carefully split in half, horizontally, using a serrated knife. Return to oven to dry out.

Assembling mocha cream hearts

Place tops of hearts on a wire rack over a tray and spread with the melted chocolate; leave to set at room temperature. Fill the bases of hearts with the mocha cream, then top with chocolate coated hearts.

Cutting hearts from coloured chocolate

Spread chocolate evenly onto baking-paper-lined tray and leave at room temperature until almost set. Carefully cut 12 x 6.5cm hearts from chocolate; refrigerate until chocolate is set.

Dipping truffles in chocolate

Allow the melted chocolate to cool slightly until it is a good coating consistency. Using two forks, quickly dip the truffles in and out of the chocolate; drain off excess chocolate, then place on a baking-paper-lined tray and refrigerate until chocolate is set.

glossary

almonds
flaked paper-thin slices.
meal also known as ground almonds.
anise also called aniseed or sweet cumin. Dried, they have a strong licorice flavour. Whole and ground seeds are available.
baking powder a raising agent consisting mainly of two parts cream of tartar to one part bicarbonate of soda (baking soda).
beetroot also known as red beets; firm, round root vegetable.
bicarbonate of soda also known as baking soda.
butter we use salted butter unless stated otherwise. Unsalted or "sweet" butter has no salt added to the churned cream.
buttermilk in spite of its name, buttermilk is actually low in fat, varying between 0.6 and 2.0 per cent per 100ml. Originally just the liquid left after cream was separated from milk, today it is commercially made similarly to yogurt. It is available from the dairy department in supermarkets.
cachous also called dragées in some countries; miniscule (3mm to 5mm) metallic-looking-but-edible confectionery balls used in cake decorating; available in silver, gold or various colours.
cardamom a spice native to India and used extensively in its cuisine; can be purchased in pod, seed or ground form. Has a distinctive aromatic, sweetly rich flavour.
chocolate
Choc Bits also called chocolate chips or chocolate morsels; available in milk, white and dark chocolate. Made of cocoa liquor, cocoa butter, sugar and an emulsifier, they hold their shape in baking and are ideal for decorating.
dark eating made of cocoa liquor, cocoa butter and sugar.
Melts small discs of compounded milk, white or dark chocolate ideal for melting and moulding.
milk eating most popular eating chocolate; mild and very sweet.
white eating contains no cocoa solids but derives its sweet flavour from cocoa butter. Very sensitive to heat.
chocolate hazelnut spread also known as Nutella.
cinnamon available in the piece (called sticks or quills) and ground. The dried inner bark of the shoots of the Sri Lankan native cinnamon tree, much of what is sold as the real thing is in fact cassia, Chinese cinnamon, from the bark of the cassia tree. It is less expensive to process than true cinnamon and is often blended with Sri Lankan cinnamon to produce the product most commonly found in supermarkets.
coco pops are chocolate-flavoured rice bubbles.
cocoa powder also called cocoa; unsweetened, dried, roasted then ground cocoa beans.

coconut, shredded unsweetened thin strips of dried coconut flesh.
coconut-flavoured liqueur we use Malibu, a coconut-flavoured rum.
coffee-flavoured liqueur use either kahlua or tia maria.
corn syrup an imported product available in some supermarkets, delicatessens and health food stores. Made from cornstarch, it is a popular ingredient in American cooking for frostings, jams and jellies.
cornflour also called cornstarch. Available made from corn or wheat (wheaten cornflour, gluten-free, gives a lighter texture in cakes).
cream cheese commonly known as philly or philadelphia; a soft cow-milk cheese, its fat content ranging from 14 to 33 per cent.
dried cranberries also called craisins; available from the dried fruit section in most supermarkets.
eggs if recipes call for raw or barely cooked eggs, exercise caution if there is a salmonella problem in your area, particularly for children and pregnant women.
figs originally from the countries that border the eastern Mediterranean; are best eaten in peak season, at the height of summer. Figs are also glacéd (candied), dried or canned in sugar syrup; these are usually sold at health-food stores, Middle Eastern food shops or specialty cheese counters.
flour
plain also known as all-purpose; made from wheat flour, it is the best for baking.
rice very fine, almost powdery, gluten-free flour; made from ground white rice.
self-raising all-purpose plain or wholemeal flour with baking powder and salt added; can be made at home with plain or wholemeal flour sifted with baking powder in the proportion of 1 cup flour to 2 teaspoons baking powder.
wholemeal also called wholewheat flour; milled with the wheat germ so is higher in fibre and more nutritional than plain flour.
gelatine we use powdered gelatine in this book; it's also available in sheet form known as leaf gelatine. Two teaspoons of powdered gelatine (7g or one sachet) is roughly equal to four gelatine leaves. The two types are interchangeable but leaf gelatine gives a clearer mixture than powdered gelatine.
ginger
ground also called powdered ginger; used as a flavouring in cakes, pies and puddings but cannot be substituted for fresh ginger.
glacé fresh ginger root preserved in sugar syrup; use crystallised ginger instead, but rinse with warm water and dry before using.
glacé fruit fruit such as pineapple, apricots, peaches and pears that are cooked in a heavy syrup and then dried.
gold leaf (edible) available from cake decorating or art supply stores.

golden syrup a by-product of refined sugarcane; pure maple syrup or honey can often be substituted.
hazelnuts also known as filberts; plump, grape-size, rich, sweet nut having a brown inedible skin that is removed by vigorously rubbing heated nuts together in a tea-towel.
meal is made by grounding the hazelnuts to a coarse floury texture and is used in baking or as a thickening agent.
kirsch is a cherry-flavoured liqueur.
macadamias native to Australia; fairly large, slightly soft, buttery rich nut. Should always be stored in the fridge to prevent their high oil content turning them rancid.
mascarpone cheese an Italian fresh cultured-cream product made in much the same way as yogurt. Whiteish to creamy yellow in colour, with a buttery-rich, luscious texture it is soft, creamy and spreadable.
milk we use full-cream homogenised milk unless otherwise specified.
full-cream powder instant powdered milk made from whole cow milk with the liquid removed and emulsifiers added.
sweetened condensed a canned milk product consisting of milk with more than half the water content removed and sugar added to the remaining milk.
orange-flavoured liqueur we use Grand Marnier, Curacao or Cointreau.
pecans native to the US and now grown locally; pecans are golden brown, buttery and rich. Good in savoury as well as sweet dishes; walnuts are a good substitute.
pistachios green, delicately flavoured nuts inside hard off-white shells. Available salted or unsalted in their shells; you can also get them shelled.
popcorn a variety of corn that is sold as kernels for popping corn, or can be bought ready-popped.
quince paste available from most supermarkets and delicatessens.
ready-rolled pastry packaged sheets of frozen shortcrust, butter puff, or puff pastry; available from supermarkets.
rhubarb a plant with long, green-red stalks; becomes sweet and edible when cooked.
sugar
brown an extremely soft, fine granulated sugar retaining molasses for its characteristic colour and flavour.
caster also called superfine or finely granulated table sugar.
icing also called confectioners' sugar or powdered sugar; pulverised granulated sugar crushed together with a small amount (about 3 per cent) of cornflour.
pure icing also called confectioners' sugar or powdered sugar, and does not contain cornflour.
raw natural brown granulated sugar.
vegetable oil any of a number of oils sourced from plant rather than animal fats.

conversion chart

measures

One Australian metric measuring cup holds approximately 250ml; one Australian metric tablespoon holds 20ml; one Australian metric teaspoon holds 5ml.

The difference between one country's measuring cups and another's is within a two- or three-teaspoon variance, and will not affect your cooking results. North America, New Zealand and the United Kingdom use a 15ml tablespoon.

All cup and spoon measurements are level. The most accurate way of measuring dry ingredients is to weigh them. When measuring liquids, use a clear glass or plastic jug with the metric markings.

We use large eggs with an average weight of 60g.

dry measures

METRIC	IMPERIAL
15g	½oz
30g	1oz
60g	2oz
90g	3oz
125g	4oz (¼lb)
155g	5oz
185g	6oz
220g	7oz
250g	8oz (½lb)
280g	9oz
315g	10oz
345g	11oz
375g	12oz (¾lb)
410g	13oz
440g	14oz
470g	15oz
500g	16oz (1lb)
750g	24oz (1½lb)
1kg	32oz (2lb)

liquid measures

METRIC	IMPERIAL
30ml	1 fluid oz
60ml	2 fluid oz
100ml	3 fluid oz
125ml	4 fluid oz
150ml	5 fluid oz (¼ pint/1 gill)
190ml	6 fluid oz
250ml	8 fluid oz
300ml	10 fluid oz (½ pint)
500ml	16 fluid oz
600ml	20 fluid oz (1 pint)
1000ml (1 litre)	1¾ pints

length measures

METRIC	IMPERIAL
3mm	⅛in
6mm	¼in
1cm	½in
2cm	¾in
2.5cm	1in
5cm	2in
6cm	2½in
8cm	3in
10cm	4in
13cm	5in
15cm	6in
18cm	7in
20cm	8in
23cm	9in
25cm	10in
28cm	11in
30cm	12in (1ft)

oven temperatures

These oven temperatures are only a guide for conventional ovens. For fan-forced ovens, check the manufacturer's manual.

	°C (CELSIUS)	°F (FAHRENHEIT)	GAS MARK
Very slow	120	250	½
Slow	150	275-300	1-2
Moderately slow	160	325	3
Moderate	180	350-375	4-5
Moderately hot	200	400	6
Hot	220	425-450	7-8
Very hot	240	475	9

index

ARE YOU MISSING SOME COOKBOOKS?

The Australian Women's Weekly Cookbooks are available from bookshops, cookshops, supermarkets and other stores all over the world. You can also buy direct from the publisher, using the order form below.

To order: Mail or fax – photocopy or complete the order form above, and send your credit card details or cheque payable to: Australian Consolidated Press (UK), ACP Books, 10 Scirocco Close, Moulton Park Office Village, Northampton NN3 6AP
phone (+44) (0)1604 642 200
fax (+44) (0)1604 642 300
email books@acpuk.com
or order online at www.acpuk.com
Non-UK residents: We accept the credit cards listed on the coupon, or cheques, drafts or International Money Orders payable in sterling and drawn on a UK bank. Credit card charges are at the exchange rate current at the time of payment.
Postage and packing UK: Add £1.00 per order plus £1.75 per book.
Postage and packing overseas: Add £2.00 per order plus £3.50 per book.
All pricing current at time of going to press and subject to change/availability.
Offer ends 31.12.2008

TITLE	RRP	QTY	TITLE	RRP	QTY
100 Fast Fillets	£6.99		Grills	£6.99	
A Taste of Chocolate	£6.99		Indian Cooking Class	£6.99	
After Work Fast	£6.99		Japanese Cooking Class	£6.99	
Beginners Cooking Class	£6.99		Just For One	£6.99	
Beginners Thai	£6.99		Just For Two	£6.99	
Best Food Fast	£6.99		Kids' Birthday Cakes	£6.99	
Breads & Muffins	£6.99		Kids Cooking	£6.99	
Brunches, Lunches & Treats	£6.99		Kids' Cooking Step-by-Step	£6.99	
Cafe Classics	£6.99		Low-carb, Low-fat	£6.99	
Cafe Favourites	£6.99		Low-fat Food for Life	£6.99	
Cakes Bakes & Desserts	£6.99		Low-fat Meals in Minutes	£6.99	
Cakes Biscuits & Slices	£6.99		Main Course Salads	£6.99	
Cakes Cooking Class	£6.99		Mexican	£6.99	
Caribbean Cooking	£6.99		Middle Eastern Cooking Class	£6.99	
Casseroles	£6.99		Mince in Minutes	£6.99	
Casseroles & Slow-Cooked Classics	£6.99		Moroccan & the Foods of North Africa	£6.99	
Cheap Eats	£6.99		Muffins, Scones & Breads	£6.99	
Cheesecakes: baked and chilled	£6.99		New Casseroles	£6.99	
Chicken	£6.99		New Curries	£6.99	
Chicken Meals in Minutes	£6.99		New Finger Food	£6.99	
Chinese and the foods of Thailand, Vietnam, Malaysia & Japan	£6.99		New French Food	£6.99	
			New Salads	£6.99	
Chinese Cooking Class	£6.99		Party Food and Drink	£6.99	
Christmas Cooking	£6.99		Pasta Meals in Minutes	£6.99	
Chocs & Treats	£6.99		Potatoes	£6.99	
Cocktails	£6.99		Quick & Simple Cooking (Apr 08)	£6.99	
Cookies & Biscuits	£6.99		Rice & Risotto	£6.99	
Cooking Class Cake Decorating	£6.99		Sauces Salsas & Dressings	£6.99	
Cupcakes & Fairycakes	£6.99		Sensational Stir-Fries	£6.99	
Detox	£6.99		Simple Healthy Meals	£6.99	
Dinner Lamb	£6.99		Simple Starters Mains & Puds	£6.99	
Easy Comfort Food (May 08)	£6.99		Soup	£6.99	
Easy Curry	£6.99		Stir-fry	£6.99	
Easy Midweek Meals	£6.99		Superfoods for Exam Success	£6.99	
Easy Spanish-Style	£6.99		Tapas Mezze Antipasto & other bites	£6.99	
Food for Fit and Healthy Kids	£6.99		Thai Cooking Class	£6.99	
Foods of the Mediterranean	£6.99		Traditional Italian	£6.99	
Foods That Fight Back	£6.99		Vegetarian Meals in Minutes	£6.99	
Fresh Food Fast	£6.99		Vegie Food	£6.99	
Fresh Food for Babies & Toddlers	£6.99		Wicked Sweet Indulgences	£6.99	
Good Food for Babies & Toddlers	£6.99		Wok Meals in Minutes	£6.99	
Great Kids' Cakes (May 08)	£6.99				
Greek Cooking Class	£6.99		TOTAL COST:	£	

Mr/Mrs/Ms _____

Address _____

_____ Postcode _____

Day time phone _____ Email* (optional) _____

I enclose my cheque/money order for £ _____

or please charge £ _____

to my: ☐ Access ☐ Mastercard ☐ Visa ☐ Diners Club

Card number [| | | | | | | | | | | | | | | |]

Expiry date _____ 3 digit security code *(found on reverse of card)* _____

Cardholder's name _____ Signature _____

* By including your email address, you consent to receipt of any email regarding this magazine, and other email inform you of ACP's other publications, products, services and events, and to promote third party goods and ser may be interested in.

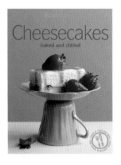

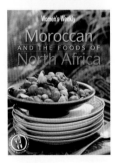

TEST KITCHEN
Food director Pamela Clark
Assistant food editors Alexandra Somerville, Sarah Schwikkard
Home economist Kellie-Marie Thomas

ACP BOOKS
General manager Christine Whiston
Editorial director Susan Tomnay
Creative director Hieu Chi Nguyen
Designer Caryl Wiggins
Senior editor Stephanie Kistner
Director of sales Brian Cearnes
Marketing manager Bridget Cody
Business analyst Ashley Davies
Operations manager David Scotto
International rights enquiries Laura Bamford
lbamford@acpuk.com

acp books

ACP Books are published by ACP Magazines
a division of PBL Media Pty Limited
Group publisher, Women's lifestyle
Pat Ingram
Director of sales, Women's lifestyle
Lynette Phillips
Commercial manager, Women's lifestyle
Seymour Cohen
Marketing director, Women's lifestyle
Matthew Dominello
Public relations manager, Women's lifestyle
Hannah Deveraux
Creative director, Events, Women's lifestyle
Luke Bonnano
Research Director, Women's lifestyle
Justin Stone
ACP Magazines, Chief Executive officer
Scott Lorson
PBL Media, Chief Executive officer
Ian Law

Produced by ACP Books, Sydney.
Published by ACP Books, a division of
ACP Magazines Ltd, 54 Park St, Sydney;
GPO Box 4088, Sydney, NSW 2001.
phone (02) 9282 8618 fax (02) 9267 9438.
acpbooks@acpmagazines.com.au
www.acpbooks.com.au
Printed by Dai Nippon in Korea.

Australia Distributed by Network Services,
phone +61 2 9282 8777 fax +61 2 9264 3278
networkweb@networkservicescompany.com.au
United Kingdom Distributed by Australian
Consolidated Press (UK),
phone (01604) 642 200 fax (01604) 642 300
books@acpuk.com
New Zealand Distributed by Netlink
Distribution Company,
phone (9) 366 9966 ask@ndc.co.nz
South Africa Distributed by PSD Promotions,
phone (27 11) 392 6065/6/7
fax (27 11) 392 6079/80
orders@psdprom.co.za
Canada Distributed by Publishers Group Canada
phone (800) 663 5714 fax (800) 565 3770
service@raincoast.com

A catalogue record for this book is available from
the British Library.
ISBN 978-1-86396-724-2
© ACP Magazines Ltd 2008
ABN 18 053 273 546

The publishers would like to thank the following
for props used in photography: Gin & Tonic;
Dedece; Macleay on Manning; Mokum; Radford
Furnishings; Third Drawer Down; Top3 by Design.

...books and more available on sale
...kshops, selected supermarkets or
...lisher (see order form page 119).

...ls which
...vices you